The
BODY

The BODY
Study Guide
By T.M. Moore

CHARLES COLSON
WITH ELLEN SANTILLI VAUGHN

WORD PUBLISHING
Dallas · London · Vancouver · Melbourne

2 3 4 5 6 7 8 9 LBM 7 6 5 4 3 2 1

Printed in the United States of America

CONTENTS

118333

Introduction

HOW TO USE THIS BOOK

This study guide is designed for group or individual use as a companion to *The Body*, by Charles W. Colson with Ellen Santilli Vaughn. It has been prepared to draw attention to the main points of the book and to facilitate biblical reflection and personal application concerning these important teachings.

Each of the guide's eight study sessions is divided into five sections: read and observe, review and reflect, respond and apply, personal learning objectives, and items for prayer.

READ AND OBSERVE

In this section readers are led to take note of the main ideas presented in each chapter of *The Body*. A marking scheme can help you keep track of ideas throughout the book. For example, you might mark in the margin notes to identify where the book discusses the nature of the church and its challenges, mission, and needs.

Nature—What is the church? What should it be? Of what does it consist?

Challenges—What are the trials, problems, and obstacles facing the church today?

Mission—How should the church respond to and serve its community?

Needs—What things need to change, or what does the church need to fulfill its mission in the world?

Use the questions in the read and observe section to lead you in your reading. If you read all the questions in this section before you read the chapters, they will help you be alert to main ideas.

REVIEW AND REFLECT

The review and reflect section looks at passages of Scripture that support, develop, or illustrate the ideas presented in the chapters you have read.

RESPOND AND APPLY

The respond and apply section includes pointed questions designed to help personalize the material you have studied. Be prepared for some hard introspection! These questions are designed to help you prepare for discussion.

PERSONAL LEARNING OBJECTIVES

Each lesson asks you to reflect on changes taking place in your life and relate them to learning objectives you establish for yourself in the first section.

ITEMS FOR PRAYER

The items for prayer section gives you an opportunity to incorporate what you are reading and learning into your daily prayer life. Here you will be provided space to list topics you wish to include in your prayers.

The Body is one of the most important books of our time. This study guide will help you to study, understand, and apply its teachings.

T. M. Moore

1

The Wretched and the Pitiful?

THE BODY, CHAPTERS 1–3

> *When compared with previous generations of believers, we seem among the most thoroughly at peace with our culture, the least adept at transforming society, and the most desperate for a meaningful faith. Our* raison d'être *is confused, our mission obscured, and our existence as a people in jeopardy.*

How well does what we know as the church match what the church should be? This question is basic to the investigations, cases, stories, recollections, and expositions of Scripture that provide the meat of what you will be reading and studying over the next several weeks. The church today has not escaped the powerful influence of what Christopher Lasch called "the culture of narcissism," and what has been variously referred to as the "me-generation," the "consumer society," and the "feel-good generation." Indeed, instead of turning our age upside-down for Jesus Christ, the church has in many ways been turned inside-out and every-which-way-but-loose by the spirit of the times! The result has been a body that is outwardly flourishing and prominent, but inwardly and in fact "wretched, pitiful, poor, blind and naked" (Rev. 3:17 NIV). In the first three chapters of *The Body* we are introduced to the great problem—and the great challenge—facing the people of God today.

READ AND OBSERVE

Read chapters 1–3 of *The Body*. Use the marking scheme described in the introduction to keep track of the key concepts and ideas explored and let the following questions guide your reading. Items in quotation marks refer to topics or ideas you will encounter in the reading. As you read these chapters, record your observations for use in the discussion of this section.

1. Describe the relationships between the churches in Riverton prior to the upheaval and between the churches and the community.

2. What were the sources of conflict that troubled the members of Riverton Community Church? Why was this situation perceived as a problem?

3. Do you see any evidence of the "virulent virus of radical individualism" at work within the churches in Riverton? In what ways?

4. Compare the motivations of pastors Conway and Killian in this situation. Who seems oriented more toward introducing an expression of the character of God into the

Riverton community? In that respect, which of the churches is more reflective of the Body of Christ, as He appears in the Gospels? In what ways?

5. Suppose your church had become caught up in the conflict described in chapter 1. Which side of the issue do you think your church would take? Why?

6. Have you ever witnessed or experienced a similar situation? Briefly explain.

7. Would you say the churches in Riverton were living "*Coram Deo*"? Why or why not?

8. List some of the things cited as evidence of the spirit of "radical individualism" in the church today.

9.   To what does the term "hot tub religion" refer? Why is it a problem? Where has it come from?

10.   What are some of the aspects of the "therapy model" of the church? What *should* be our model of the church?

11.   Review your answers to questions 1 through 10 and the notes you wrote in the margins of *The Body*. In a few phrases, summarize the problem that exists in the church today in terms of the problem described in chapters 1–3.

REVIEW AND REFLECT
Read Revelation 3:14–22. The following questions can help you discover the deeper meaning of this passage and reflect on the message of chapters 1–3 of *The Body*.

1.   How does Jesus explain a "lukewarm" church (v. 17)?

2. In verse 18 Jesus speaks of a "hot" church. What would a "hot" church—a church on fire, we might say—look like?

To what do the following terms refer?

Refined gold (Ps. 19:7–10):

Become rich (1 Tim. 6:17, 18):

White garments (Eph. 4:17–24):

Eye salve (Eph. 1:15–21):

3. Rewrite the letter in Revelation (vv. 14–18) following the passage's outline and ideas but addressing it *specifically* to Riverton Community Church.

4. How might Jesus "reprove and discipline" (v. 21) "lukewarm" churches in our day?

RESPOND AND REPLY
Prayerfully consider following the questions as you prepare to discuss chapters 1–3 of *The Body*.

1. As you read about the churches in Riverton, about "radical individualism," "lukewarmness," and the "therapy" view of the church, were you able to identify any aspects of these conditions in your own experience as a Christian and a church member? Explain.

2. Imagine that your church (where you currently worship) received the letter Jesus sent to the Laodiceans in Revelation 3:14–22 and that you were commissioned to write the response. What would you say? Include information about the situation in your church and in your own Christian life.

PERSONAL LEARNING OBJECTIVES
Now that you have a feel for the topics *The Body* explores, what do you hope to gain from this study? In what ways would you like to grow as a believer? How would you like to see your church become "hotter" for the Lord? How would you like to see your own experience in the church enriched?

Chapter 1

ITEMS FOR PRAYER FROM CHAPTERS 1–3

2

Candles in Their Hands

THE BODY, CHAPTERS 4–7

"I don't mind so much the loss of my leg. After all, it was I who lit the first candle." . . . God works as He will to overcome our rebellion. Like the wind that blows through the trees, He can neither be seen nor directed. He touches the heart. He breathes through snowflakes. The point is He does it. He calls people to Himself, conceiving the new life in the Spirit in the secret place of the soul.

If our churches are going to overcome the effects of the radical individualism of our day and get on with the work to which God has called them, as church members we need to make certain that our understanding of the church is consistent with what God has revealed in His Word. We must begin at the beginning, with a view of the church that is broad enough to do justice to the varieties of human cultural expression and the mysterious workings of a sovereign God, and specific enough to allow us to know exactly where we fit in the larger scheme of things. Chapters 4–7 of *The Body* can help us begin to recover this biblical understanding of the church of our Lord Jesus Christ.

READ AND OBSERVE

Read chapters 4–7 of *The Body*. Continue to mark the margins to help you stay focused on the main ideas in the book. As you read, record your answers to the questions that follow. Words in quotation marks refer to ideas you will encounter in your reading.

1. List the character traits displayed by the church members of Timisoara as they responded to the calls for renewal from Pastor Tokes.

2. What seems to have motivated Pastor Tokes in this situation? Do you see in his actions more a reflection of Pastor Killian or Pastor Conway (discussed in chapter 1)? Explain.

3. What is the significance of the "candle episode"? What does it teach us about how the church accomplishes the Kingdom purposes of Christ?

4. This portion of *The Body* emphasizes the biblical teaching that the church is first and foremost *people*. How

does this understanding compare to what most people think of when they think of the church?

5. In what sense is the church to be a "new community"? What kind of commitment does this require of church members?

6. What is the difference between the "church universal" and the "church particular"?

7. In which of these—church universal or church particular—do church members have their membership? What does this require of us?

8. What did the idea of the "communion of the saints" mean for the members of the early church? How would you describe the state of that idea today—in the church universal and in your own church?

9. What is the difference between the "church of fact" and the "church of faith"? How can this distinction help us develop and sustain our commitment to the church?

10. Irina Ratushinskaya has a clear and undoubted testimony of faith in Jesus Christ. In addition, her life clearly shows that she takes her profession of faith seriously. Her road to faith, however, may seem strange and unfamiliar to us. Below, in the column on the left, outline the steps by which Irina came to know that she had saving faith and a personal relationship with Jesus Christ. Label each step in a general way (e.g., awareness of sin, full assurance). In the middle column write a word or phrase beside each step listed, or group several steps together with a common label.

Irina's steps	Description	Your steps

In the right column, next to the labels you put on Irina's steps, list similar steps in your own journey to faith. Are there any similarities between your journey to saving faith and Irina's?

REVIEW AND REFLECT

Let's take a closer look at some passages of Scripture that can help us understand the nature of the church.

1. Take a few minutes to read Ephesians 2:14–22. What does this passage say Christ has done for those who have received His message of peace?

2. How are those who have received the message of peace through Christ related to one another (v. 19)? How does this relate to what is referred to in chapters 4–7 as "the communion of the saints"?

3. The building metaphor is often used to help us understand the church. Let's look at it more closely.

To what does the phrase, "foundation of the apostles and prophets" refer? What does it mean to have been "built upon" this foundation?

In a building, the cornerstone laid on the foundation points the way to the proper edification—horizontally and vertically—of the rest of the building. Why is this a good way to think about Christ and His relationship to the church?

How are the members of the church to be "fitted together and growing together" in the church? (See also 1 Cor. 12:4–7 and 1 Pet. 4:10, 11.)

What kind of building is it to be? Who should be seen dwelling in the church?

4. Three passages that describe how different individuals became members of the church by coming to faith in Jesus Christ are Acts 9:1–19, Acts 10:23–48, and Acts 16:22–33. Read these passages and tell how each situation is different. How are they the same?

5. Read Hebrews 12:18–24. Does this passage speak of coming to the "church particular" or the "church universal"?

What does it say is the single criterion of membership in this expression of the church (v. 24)?

RESPOND AND APPLY

As you prepare to discuss chapters 4–7 of *The Body,* spend some time reflecting on the questions that follow. Think honestly and carefully about how you might begin to apply the teachings of this part of the book.

1. Imagine that a crisis of major proportions erupted in your community—perhaps a weather disaster or the closing of a major employer that affects a large percentage of the population. Do you think the churches in your community would respond to this crisis like the churches in Timisoara did? Why or why not? Would you feel compelled to draw your church into a relief effort?

2. Think about your own journey to saving faith. What were the incidents and who were the people most responsible for helping you come to a saving knowledge of Jesus Christ?

Take some time right now to thank the Lord for how He worked to bring you to His Son. Then, write a note of appreciation and praise to God to each of the individuals who helped you come to saving faith.

3. We have seen how Irina and several biblical characters came to saving faith in Jesus Christ. What about your friends in your own church? Do you know how they came to know the Lord? Make a point to begin taking the time to let others tell you the wonderful and joyous story of how they came to saving faith. And tell your story to them, as well.

PERSONAL LEARNING OBJECTIVES

Review the personal learning objectives you wrote in Session 1 of this study guide. In what ways have you begun to make progress toward those objectives? Are you gaining any new or better perspectives on the church? Do you feel any new and welcome attitudes beginning to develop? Have any new courses of action suggested themselves?

ITEMS FOR PRAYER FROM CHAPTERS 4–7

3

Endeavoring to Keep the Unity of the Spirit

THE BODY, CHAPTERS 8–11

Harmony and oneness in spirit can be achieved only when Christians put aside their personal agendas and submit themselves to the authority of the Holy Spirit. For the Holy Spirit, which empowers the church, can never lead believers into disunity. . . . The apostle Paul gives a wonderful snapshot of what the world should see in our community as a precursor of what is to come. "For the kingdom of God is not eating and drinking, but righteousness and peace and joy in the Holy Spirit." [Rom. 14:17]

The unbelieving world around us is full of strife, jealousy, anger, and resentment. People from every walk of life seek to maximize any advantage they hold over others. The people of the world are eager for some relief from this madness, and they should be able to find it in the church of Jesus Christ. But when the church is more a mirror of the disunity of the world than the unity of the Godhead, the unbelieving world sees little to be attracted to in its "fellowship." Session 3 examines the crucial question of the unity of the Body of Christ, which is the result of the work of His Spirit in our midst.

READ AND OBSERVE

Read chapters 8–11 of *The Body*. Continue to mark in the margins as in the previous sections. As you read, the questions that follow can help you identify the main ideas in this portion of the book.

1. How did the account of the strife in Emmanuel Baptist Church make you feel? How could such a situation have arisen?

2. According to these chapters, about what things do Christians tend to disagree? Are any of these valid?

3. What is church unity? Why is unity in the church so important?

4. Is there a difference between unity and doctrinal agreement on all points? Explain.

5. What kind of unity should we be working for at the level of the church universal? Why is C. S. Lewis's phrase "mere Christianity" a good one to use here?

6. What kind of unity must we work for at the level of the church particular? How can we maintain this kind of unity while allowing for diversity in the larger Body of Christ?

7. What is the "rule of faith"? How can this be helpful in fostering church unity?

8. List the steps that must be taken to begin developing true unity in the Body of Christ. How might these steps be implemented in your church? In the churches in your community?

9. What must be the role of God's truth in working to achieve unity among the churches of Christ?

10. Why did Jonathan Edwards' sermon have such a powerful effect on the people of Enfield?

11. Explain the following in your own words: "The power of the Word. It is the heart of the church's mission."

12. Describe the two forms the ministry of the Word takes. How would you differentiate between them?

13. What is the responsibility of those who are charged with preaching the Word? What kinds of things must this person guard against in order to be faithful to this charge?

14. Who is responsible for teaching the Word? How must they use this calling?

15. How does the "therapeutic model" of the church jeopardize the ministry of the Word?

16. What are the "marks" of a true church? Briefly explain each of these.

17. How can holding fast to these "marks" of the church help us foster the unity of the Spirit in the bonds of peace?

REVIEW AND REFLECT

Let's take a closer look at a passage of Scripture that is basic to chapters 8–11. Read Ephesians 4:1–16.

1. According to vv. 1 and 2, what is Paul about to talk about in this passage?

2. Paul seems to be saying that if we do what he exhorts us to in vv. 1 and 2, we will accomplish what he hopes for in v. 3. What is that?

3. Let us rephrase what Paul says. Complete the following sentence: In order to see the unity of Christ's Body in our church and among the churches in our community, we as Christians must . . .

Compare your answer here with your answer to question 8 in the read and observe section. What parallels do you find?

4. Paul says we must "be diligent" or "make every effort" to preserve the unity of the Body. The Greek word here translates to "work hard." Why do we have to work so hard to achieve and maintain unity in the church? What kinds of things are working against us?

5. According to vv. 4–6, what is the basis for our unity in the Body?

How does Paul introduce the notion of diversity within this unity in vv. 7–11? How should our diversity and our unity work together (v. 12)?

6. We will know that our unity and diversity are working together in the Body of Christ—in the particular and the universal—when two things take place. The first is mentioned in v. 12. Define this in your own words.

The second is described in vv. 13–16 where Paul clarifies what he means by "the building up of the Body of Christ." List the indicators of a Body that is being built up.

RESPOND AND APPLY

Prayerfully consider the following questions as you prepare to discuss chapters 8–11 of *The Body*.

1. Review your answers to the questions in the first two sections of this session and your margin notes. What is required of each believer if there is to be true unity in the Body of Christ?

Are you "working hard" to preserve the unity of the Spirit in the bond of peace? How could you begin to be more effective at this challenge?

2. Are there churches in your community that would share with your church in confessing the rule of faith? Try to find out before the next discussion period.

Recall the examples and the guidelines in your reading. What are some ways your church could begin to take the lead in your community to bring the unity of Christ's Body to light before the watching world?

PERSONAL LEARNING OBJECTIVES

Review the personal learning objectives you established in Session 1. Have the readings and study questions in this session helped you to make progress toward your goals? Is there any evidence of growth—new understanding, changed attitudes, or new behavioral patterns? Where do you need to be working harder toward achieving your learning objectives?

ITEMS FOR PRAYER FROM CHAPTERS 8–11

4

One Word of Truth

THE BODY, CHAPTERS 12–15

During His ministry, Jesus made many remarkable claims. That He and His Father were one. That He could forgive sin. That through faith in Him one has life eternal. Christianity itself rests on the astonishing claim that Jesus rose bodily from the dead and ascended into heaven. But of all these claims, the most remarkable is His bold statement: I am the truth.

Perhaps the single philosophical idea people in our society hold in common is that there are no absolute truths. The institutionalization of this relativistic world view continues, leaving behind it a wake of confusion, uncertainty, and anxiety. Denying truth in the name of truth, our contemporaries are left without a firm foundation for the decisions and choices they must make every day. Because there is no final truth in the land, every person is left to do what is right in his or her own eyes. In chapters 12–15 we see why Jesus' remarkable claim to be *the Truth* needs so desperately to be heard in our day.

READ AND OBSERVE

Read chapters 12–15 of *The Body*. Continue to use the marking scheme to keep track of main ideas and key points. The following questions can help guide your reading.

1. In the face of Jesus' claim, how would Pilate most likely have understood the idea of truth? For Pilate, a Roman bureaucrat, what was the final determiner of "what is truth"?

2. How did this view of truth trap Pilate into a decision he might not otherwise have made?

3. Before continuing your reading, look at Acts 2:22–24. In Session 4 we examine the false views of truth that are widespread in our society. With the prevalence of the relativistic view of truth in the world today, we might be led to despair of ever seeing anything good come to light. But, according to this passage, our sovereign God is able to use even the false views of truth held by sinful men—like Pilate—to accomplish His good purposes. Explain.

4. What kinds of things are involved in Jesus' claim to be the Truth? What does this claim imply about His relationship to the world around us? What does it mean for our ability to understand the world and all the reality in it?

5. Where do modern men and women seek ultimate truth? How does this represent a departure from the history of Western civilization?

6. In these chapters, talk-show programs are represented as being the embodiment of modern society's approach to truth. How can we see this? Use the following phrases to help you respond.

You and you only:

The "banality" of life:

No objective moral distinctions:

7. What is the effect of this "trivializing of truth" on human experience in our society?

8. Who are the "Goodmanites"? How does their view of truth add to the confusion created by the "Donahueites'" view of truth?

9. Summarize each of the following characteristics of the relativistic world view of today's society.

Secularism:

Anti-historicism:

Naturalism:

Utopianism:

Pragmatism:

10. In such a society, what does confessing Christ as Lord involve?

11. What are the implications of the church being the "custodian and defender" of the Truth for the work of evangelism?

12. What steps can we take to renew our commitment to the Truth?

13. What is "fundamentalism," in the original sense of the word? Why is this a label we can wear with confidence?

14. In what sense must confrontation be part of our strategy for recovering a commitment to the Truth?

15. How does Mr. Abercrombie's experience illustrate the point that "conviction must precede conversion"? How does this relate to the need for confrontation in our day?

16. What is meant by the phrase "a biblical world view"? What is our responsibility for a biblical world view? How does a biblical world view compare with the relativistic world view of our day?

17. What does it mean to "be ready to give a defense of our faith"? Why must this be part of our strategy for recovering a commitment to the Truth?

18. Why is it important that Christians begin to "contend for our view of truth in the market place"? What does this mean?

REVIEW AND REFLECT
Let's look a little more carefully at some of the biblical material related to the battle for truth.

1. Look at John 19:36 and 37. What was Jesus' point of reference for His understanding of what was happening to Him? What does this say about His view of truth? That is, to what must people be willing to defer if they are to

have a true perspective on events, experiences, situations, or courses of action?

2.   According to Jesus' final remark in v. 37, what is the essential criterion for being able to be in touch with truth? In our relativistic society, where does the only hope for a recovery of truth lie?

3.   In 2 Corinthians 10:3–5, Paul tells us how he understood his obligation to the Truth in his own day. Comment briefly on the meaning of each of the following phrases.

Speculations raised up against the knowledge of God:

Destroying those speculations with divine weapons (see Eph. 6:10–19):

Taking every thought captive:

Making every thought obedient to Christ:

Now, consider your responsibility as an "imitator of Paul" (1 Cor. 4:16; 11:1). What things do you need to prepare for battle? How will that battle begin? What must be your objective? Consider the following:

Your home and family:

Your community:

Your workplace:

Your church:

4. The following passages give good advice about how we must approach the battle for the Truth. Summarize the teaching of each.

Romans 12:1, 2

Colossians 2:8

Colossians 3:16, 17

2 Timothy 2:15

1 Peter 1:13

1 Peter 3:15

1 John 4:1–3

RESPOND AND APPLY

Prayerfully consider the following exercises and questions as you prepare to discuss chapters 12–15 of *The Body*.

1. How do you assess your own state of readiness to begin engaging in the battle to recover truth?

1   2   3   4   5   6   7   8   9   10
Definitely not ready   *At a high state of readiness*

Explain your answer.

2. List the steps you could take to arm yourself for this struggle. Imagine that one year from today you will present the biblical view of truth (as opposed to the relativistic world view) to a packed meeting of the local PTA. How will you prepare? (Do not describe what you would say, but how you would begin today to prepare for this opportunity.)

PERSONAL LEARNING OBJECTIVES

Review the personal learning objectives you established back in Session 1 of this study guide. Be prepared to share with your discussion group (or with a friend if you are not part of a discussion group) how you feel you are progressing toward attaining your goals. What is standing in the way of even greater progress?

ITEMS FOR PRAYER FROM CHAPTERS 12–15

5

Reformers Then and Now

THE BODY, CHAPTERS 16–19

"Mikhail Sergeyevich!" one of the priests shouted, his deep voice cleaving the clamor of the protesters and piercing straight toward the angry Soviet leader. "Mikhail Sergeyevich! Christ is risen!" In a matter of months after that final May Day celebration, the Soviet Union was officially dissolved. Christ is risen indeed and is building His church, ". . . and the gates of hell shall not prevail against it."

The dramatic events in Eastern Europe over the last several years echo the dramatic events of four-and-a-half centuries ago when believers with deep-seated convictions determined to stand up for what they believed—against all odds and at all costs. Yet the question remains as to whether churches in the evangelical West will be ignited by the spirit of renewal as were their brethren in the East. In chapters 16–19 of *The Body* we are challenged by the courage of our fellow believers, then and now, to take our place in the continuing reformation of the church.

READ AND OBSERVE
Read chapters 16–19 of *The Body*. Use the following questions to guide you.

1. In how many different ways can you see that the Holy Spirit was working among the people of God in Eastern Europe during the years of Soviet oppression?

2. How did the mainline churches in this country succumb to the temptation of politics? What did it cost them?

3. In what ways are evangelicals being similarly tempted?

4. To what does the word "accommodation" refer in this section of *The Body*? Can you see evidence of accommodation in the life of your church? In your own faith?

5. To what does the phrase "politically correct" refer? In what ways has it begun to characterize certain sectors of the evangelical church? What is the danger in this?

6. As Christians, how do we experience pressure to conform to the culture and society around us?

7. Trace the progression of Luther's awakening to Christ. In what ways was his journey like Irina's? (Refer to chapter 6 of *The Body*.) How was his journey like your own?

8. What did Luther come to see that changed him?

9. To what does the biblical idea of "justice" refer? How does justice relate to "the mystery of God's plan for His people"?

10. What was the Reformation? Why is it important to us today?

11. How did the Reformation affect the following?

Politics and government:

The view of work:

Economics:

Education:

Science:

Art:

The church:

12. In what ways have Catholic and Protestant dogma begun to converge in our day?

REVIEW AND REFLECT

Read Acts 4. This passage can give us much-needed insight into how we, following the example of the early reformers and our brethren in Eastern Europe, must begin to stand up, with greater boldness, for what we believe.

1. In Acts 4:1–10, what seems to have been the cause of the problem? Why were the apostles hauled into court?

2. Explain how Peter was not the least bit "accommodating" in his testimony to the court (vv. 11, 12).

3. What caused the members of the court to marvel (v. 13)? What is the significance of this for us today?

4. What warning was given to the apostles? How did they respond (vv. 14–20)?

5. When the apostles returned to the church to report on the situation, how did he know that the people were afraid of what might happen? (Look at what they prayed for in v. 29.)

6. How did the people keep their fear from letting them accommodate the demands of their persecutors? On what is their prayer based?

7. Taking a cue from these early believers, how can we learn to stand up against the threats and intimidations of the surrounding culture? Where should we begin?

RESPOND AND APPLY

Prayerfully consider the following questions as you prepare to discuss chapters 16–19 of *The Body."*

1. Reflect on the example of the sixteenth-century reformers, the believers in Eastern Europe, and the early church in Acts 4. What do you consider to be the most important things for you to learn?

2. In what ways are you threatened with "accommodating" to the *spiritus mundi?* How can the example of the believers we have discussed in this session provide you strength to stand firm for the ultimate truth of Jesus Christ?

3. How can you encourage your fellow believers to awaken to the need for reformation and renewal in our day?

PERSONAL LEARNING OBJECTIVES

Review your personal learning objectives for this study. Can you see any evidence that you are beginning to change your view of the church? In your understanding of your role in the church? Do you recognize areas you need to change but where you are still struggling? Share these with a friend and ask for prayer support that you might continue to grow.

ITEMS FOR PRAYER FROM CHAPTERS 16–19

6

Greater Things

"I tell you the truth," said Jesus to the followers gathered at the Passover table, "anyone who has faith in me will do what I have been doing." The disciples must have looked at one another in bewilderment. They had seen the Master cast out demons and raise the dead. How could they possibly do that? But then their Teacher went even further, adding, "He will do greater things than these, because I am going to the Father." Greater things than these? . . . What in the world was He talking about?

Most of us in the evangelical world do not suffer from holding expectations too high. If anything, our vision of what we have been called to in this world could use some serious stretching! Jesus' expectations of the impact His disciples would make on the world around them must have startled them, until they began to see those expectations actually come to pass. Chapters 20–22 of *The Body* examine the church's mission in our dying age.

READ AND OBSERVE
Read chapters 20–22 of *The Body.* Continue to make notes in the margins as recommended in the introduction so you can keep track of the key concepts and main

ideas in the book. Let the questions that follow guide your reading.

1. In what sense should the followers of Christ expect to do greater things than He did? How can this be?

2. What does it mean that the church must first *be* the church before it can carry out the mission of the church?

3. In what sense is the church's call to make disciples more than just a call to evangelism?

4. What are the indications of a healthy, growing church?

5. What is the role of each of the following in bringing God's truth to the world?

Pastors:

The laity:

6. What does it mean to be a "disciplined" people of God?

7. How should the church equip its members?

8. List the ways your church equips its members.

9. What is the "celebrity syndrome"? How has this affected the evangelical church? Describe any examples you have seen.

10. What is meant by the "pedestal complex"? What problems have arisen as a result of the celebrity syndrome and the pedestal complex?

11. What kind of leadership model did Jesus give to oppose these? How does this model differ from the pedestal complex and the celebrity syndrome?

12. What steps must churches take to implement the servant-leadership model?

REVIEW AND REFLECT

To help us get a better picture of what we need to be and do in our generation, let's look at the early church as it began to carry out its mission to the lost world of its day.

1. Read Acts 2:37–42. How did the people of Jerusalem respond to the first evangelistic sermon? How did the church respond to them? What evidence do you see that a new community was emerging?

2. Read Acts 2:43–47. How did Christ's life affect these believers? How did their neighbors respond to what they saw?

3. Acts 4:29–31 shows the conclusion of the situation we examined earlier. Who was doing the work of evangelism, and how were they enabled to do it?

4. How does Acts 4:32–37 show that new believers coming to Christ were being incorporated into the life of the Body according to the pattern established in Acts 2:42–47?

5. When Barnabas was sent to Antioch to inspect the goings-on there, what must he have seen that convinced him that this new congregation was truly part of the Body of Christ (Acts 11:19–24)?

RESPOND AND APPLY

Prayerfully consider the following questions as you prepare to discuss the material in chapters 20–22 of *The Body.*

1. To what extent has your congregation been involved in doing the "greater things" that Jesus promised?

1   **2**   **3**   **4**   **5**   **6**   **7**   **8**   **9**   **10**

Not significantly   *To a very great extent*

Explain.

2. Have you seen any evidence of the celebrity syndrome, the pedestal complex, or the servant-leadership model in your church? Describe. How could you encourage more of the servant-leadership model and less of the other two?

3. What obstacles keep your church from accomplishing the "greater things" that Jesus promised?

PERSONAL LEARNING OBJECTIVES

Review your learning objectives for this study. In which areas do you have the most difficulty growing or changing? Why do you think this is so? Find a friend who will pray with you and for you as you continue working on these areas of your life.

ITEMS FOR PRAYER FROM CHAPTERS 20–22

7

Who Are You?

THE BODY, CHAPTERS 23–25

For the first and last time, the commandant looks Kolbe in the eye. "Who are you?" he asks. The prisoner looks back at him, a strange fire in his dark eyes.

Scripture tells us that believers were first called Christians in Antioch (Acts 11:26). This was probably because their conversation and lives witnessed to their faith in Him. He was all they could talk about—the explanation for their every good deed, the rationale for their boundless hope, the reason for their new-found joy, the conclusion of their every conversation. His was the name they gladly invoked when asked by their curious and befuddled neighbors, "Who is your teacher?" And, glad for the epithet bestowed on them, they gladly owned up to the charges of their contemporaries when asked, "Who are you?" Chapters 23–25 of *The Body* focus on what that question means to us as followers of Jesus Christ.

READ AND OBSERVE

Read chapters 23–25 of *The Body*. Use the questions that follow to guide you.

1. What is the moral of the Father Kolbe story? On what points can you identify with Father Kolbe?

2. Describe the meaning of this statement: "Being witnesses involves every aspect of what we are and do, individually and collectively, as the community of faith."

3. To whom has the responsibility for the work of evangelism been given?

4. What is the primary context in which God's people should be doing the work of evangelism?

5. What is meant by the term "post-Christian culture"? Can you see any evidence of post-Christian culture in your community?

6. What do we have in common with the early believers when it comes to the work of evangelism?

7. Why must evangelism always be connected to the local church?

8. In what sense are the followers of Jesus Christ the light of the world?

9. How do the stories of Annie, Sherry, Melissa, Beverly and Jackie, and John illustrate the principle of the church as the light of the world?

REVIEW AND REFLECT

Let's look at this idea of the church serving as the light of the world. Use the following questions as a guide.

1. In Matthew 5:14–16, Jesus pictures His followers as the light of the world. What does He say cannot be true of those who are the light of the world?

2. Based on what you have learned from your study of *The Body*, as well as what you know about our world, how effectively is the church fulfilling its call to give light to all men? Explain your answer.

3. There is something very intentional, very determined, about the action of placing the light on the lampstand as mentioned in Matthew 5:15. How should that picture guide the church to be the light of Christ in the community?

4. What are some things that must occur if your church is going to become more effective in bringing the light of Christ to the community?

5. How will you know when your light-bearing is truly effective? What answer is suggested in v. 16? In practical terms, what would that look like?

6. Consider yourself and the other members of your discussion group. Where should the light of Christ be shining in your community? Is it?

RESPOND AND APPLY

Review your margin notes and your answers to the questions above. Then prayerfully consider the following questions as you prepare to discuss chapters 23–25.

1. How effectively are you serving as a source of Christ's light in your everyday life?

1	2	3	4	5	6	7	8	9	10
Very ineffective							*Highly effective*		

Explain your answer.

2. What do you need to become a more effective and more consistent witness for Christ? Does your church offer this?

3. How could the members of your discussion group begin to help one another grow as witnesses for Christ? Are you willing to make a plan and enter into a covenant to do so?

PERSONAL LEARNING OBJECTIVES

Take some time to praise the Lord in prayer and song for the ways He has helped you grow through this study. Ask Him to show you areas you still need to change. Ask Him to make you willing to change, and praise Him in advance for the continuing growth that He will bring.

ITEMS FOR PRAYER FROM CHAPTERS 23–25

8

Salt Parables

THE BODY, CHAPTERS 26–29

The church as salt is not only a biblical mandate, it is also particularly applicable in our modern world. . . . But, as a general strategy, we will be more effective when we penetrate behind the lines, influencing the culture from within—which, by the way, does not mean we lose our character. Salt is still salt.

The unbelievers in Thessalonica complained that the Christians were turning the world upside-down (Acts 17:6). Actually, they would have been more accurate to say that they were turning it inside-out and right-side-up! They were able to accomplish this because they understood the principle of salt—that is, that the people of Christ are the salt of the world. As we examine this principle in the final section of *The Body*, let us find examples of people living the salt principle parables for us and our churches in this post-Christian world.

READ AND OBSERVE
Read chapters 26–29 of *The Body*. As you read, look for ways the stories told here can serve as parables for you, your church, and the evangelical community.

1. What aspects of the life and ministry of the church are illustrated in the story of Tom Phillips?

2. Why is salt a particularly good metaphor for thinking about the church's existence and calling in the world?

3. What is the principle of "infiltration"? How can believers use this principle?

4. How does Circle Urban illustrate the principle of the Body as salt?

5. What does being salt require of us?

6.　How do Amy Grant and Joe Gibbs exemplify this salt principle?

7.　In what sense must each of us begin to see ourselves as ministers of the gospel?

8.　What does it mean to "know the fear of the Lord"? Why does this seem to be so needed in the church today?

9.　How is the story of Rusty and Bob a parable of the church in our modern world? What does it suggest about the absence of truth in our society? About the lostness of modern men and women? About the power of the gospel? The unity of believers? The nature of evangelism and discipleship? The battle for truth? The church as light and salt?

REVIEW AND REFLECT

Let's look at one of the "saltiest dogs" in all of Scripture—Daniel!

1. In Daniel 1:1–15, how did Daniel make it clear to his Babylonian captors that he was not going to accommodate their religious convictions? How did God bless that?

2. In Daniel 2:1–16 Nebuchadnezzar felt a certain way because of a particular need he encountered. How did he feel, and what was his need?

3. In 2:16–18 Daniel makes himself available to meet that need. What was he going to do, and where did he find the wherewithal to do it?

4. As Daniel met the king's need, how did Nebuchadnezzar respond (Dan. 2:46–49)? Is this response different from his attitude toward God in 1:1 and 2?

5. Look at Nebuchadnezzar's response to the coura-geous stance of Daniel's friends in Daniel 3:28–30. Do you see any more movement in the king in this response?

6. Now look at the way Nebuchadnezzar responded after Daniel called him to repentance and he experienced God's judgment of his pride and his indifference to the suffering around him (Dan. 4:34–37). How did Daniel in-terpret the king's "profession of faith" (Dan. 5:18–22)?

7. What led Nebuchadnezzar from being a despiser of God to a worshiper of God? How do these factors relate to the principle of salt we have been examining?

RESPOND AND APPLY

As you prepare to discuss chapters 26–29 of *The Body*, consider the following questions.

1. What areas of your community can you "salt" in your everyday life? Discuss these areas with your discus-sion group.

2. In what areas of your community is salt very much needed?

3. How might the ministries of your church be used to encourage greater saltiness on the part of church members?

4. What will you need if you are to become more effective in fulfilling your own role as salt in the community?

PERSONAL LEARNING OBJECTIVES

Review all the learning objectives you set during this course. Carefully evaluate your progress. For what kinds of growth or changes can you give God the praise? Where do you still need to keep working? How will you follow up on this study and continue to grow as a member of the Body of Christ?

ITEMS FOR PRAYER FROM CHAPTERS 26–29